# YOU
## WERE BORN
### *to be*
# Healthy

D1602662

DEAR Sarah,

AN HONOR & Pleasure
to share the TEDx
stage with you.

Keep your fire
lit.

# YOU
## WERE BORN
### *to be*
# Healthy

OTTO JANKE, DC

ARCHWAY
PUBLISHING

Archway Publishing books may be ordered through booksellers or by contacting:

Archway Publishing
1663 Liberty Drive
Bloomington, IN 47403
www.archwaypublishing.com
1-(888)-242-5904

Because of the dynamic nature of the Internet, any web addresses or links contained in this book may have changed since publication and may no longer be valid. The views expressed in this work are solely those of the author and do not necessarily reflect the views of the publisher, and the publisher hereby disclaims any responsibility for them.

Any people depicted in stock imagery provided by Thinkstock are models, and such images are being used for illustrative purposes only.

Certain stock imagery © Thinkstock.

ISBN: 978-1-4808-0080-9 (sc)
ISBN: 978-1-4808-0081-6 (e)
Library of Congress Control Number: 2013907581

Printed in the United States of America

Archway Publishing rev. date: 5/3/2013

# TABLE OF CONTENTS

# YOU WERE BORN TO BE HEALTHY

You were born with everything you have ever needed to be healthy or to learn to be healthy.

For every disease with which man has come in contact, no matter how devastating, from the Black Death to HIV to the scourge of modern man, cancer, there has been someone, somewhere who has beat it. There has *always* been someone who beat it. There always will be someone who beats it.

In the mid-1990s, I had the great pleasure to work with a patient who was HIV positive. She came in on a Saturday morning, the same way she had for the last eight months. She was particularly bubbly this Saturday morning. I asked her why the bubbles, and she said, "Oh, I am just in a good mood."

I asked again, "Why?"

"Just a good mood, that's all."

But it wasn't all. It was much more than just a good mood. So I said, "You know the rules. If you can tell me all the bad stuff, then you have to tell me the good stuff too."

"Well, my blood work came back and my T-cell count is up."

"Congratulations," I said. "But why would your T-cell count have been down?" (T-cell counts are a way to judge the strength of your immune system.)

"I'm HIV positive, and this is the first time in five years that my count has gone up."

Holy smokes. I had not known previous to this moment that she was HIV positive. And it was the mid-1990s, and I was not sure if I should Lysol the room or go wash my hands. I asked, "Why do you think the count went up?" I thought it was a good question, and I really wanted to know. We had been inundated with all the bad news about HIV, and it was considered a curse of death if you were diagnosed with it.

"I have been thinking about that for the last few days since I got the results, and the only thing I have done differently in the last years is  ,… and she looked me straight in the eyes and said "come here and get adjusted by you." *Wow.* I said to myself, *Holy crap! This stuff really works.* Let me get something straight: I don't cure anybody of anything—I am incapable of doing that. Only the body cures itself. I just happen to help it.

I was genuinely stunned. HIV had been such a death sentence for so many. So to see and hear that this young girl had actually improved her immune system sent my head racing. I called Palmer College of Chiropractic and asked them if they had heard about people with HIV being helped with chiropractic adjustments. They said that preliminary research was indeed very positive. I called Life College of Chiropractic and spoke with Dr. John Grostic, who also agreed that research was showing it can help with HIV.

This led me to the National Institute of Health (NIH) and to the Centers for Disease Control and Prevention (CDC) to see what they were saying. It was during many hours logged into the net that I read what Dr. Robert Fauci of the NIH said about HIV and our bodies. To paraphrase, he said that we already have everything that we need to control and conquer HIV.

We already have everything we need to beat HIV, but we haven't seen it happen yet. HIV was unlike the flu. We can count on seeing the flu every year. But HIV was new to humans, so how could we have everything we need to beat something that we have never even seen before? A simplified explanation points to the relationship between nature and nurture.

## God vs. Darwin

It doesn't matter if you are a creationist or an evolutionist. In either case, you have to believe that we are born to be healthy.

If you follow the evolutionary model that humans started as an amino acid bouillabaisse and that we have reached our top rung on the animal ladder through positive mutations along millions of generations, then how did we get this far without having the makeup to naturally be healthy? As a species, we wouldn't have been able to get here unless there was an inborn blueprint for health. Why on earth would we have an inborn genetic makeup for disease? This just does not make any sense. Do any other species have an inborn genetic makeup for disease? No.

And if you are a creationist, in that God created the earth and man, and that we are created in his likeness, then why on earth would he have made us anything but healthy? Is it because he has some sick sense of humor and he likes to see certain people suffer? No. Just like our tomato plants, our dogs, and everything else, we are born to be healthy.

## It's your choice

When I raise this point to an audience, someone always asks, "So then why are so many people unhealthy?" I am not talking about birth defects that some people are born with; I am talking about the vast majority of Americans who are slowly dying as they speed up the aging process.

So why are so many people unhealthy? We are unhealthy because we choose to be. It is really that simple. We make this choice everyday by choosing what we do, don't do, eat, don't eat, think, don't think, take, and don't take. We will return to this idea later in the book.

If we have a choice to be unhealthy, then it should be very obvious that we also have the option to be as healthy as we want to be. And it doesn't matter what health status you are at, you can always be a little bit better. You were born with the ability to be healthy—you just need to unlock it, unleash it, and let it rock.

# Chapter 1

# THE AMERICAN PARADOX

There is a term in health care called "the French paradox." This term refers to a country that has a higher saturated fat content in its foods and higher smoking rates than America, but only a fraction of the heart disease.

So let's examine the American paradox. Shouldn't the country that spends by far the most on health care per person also be the country where its residents live the longest? Shouldn't that country be by far the healthiest in the world? Logic would certainly imply the validity of these ideas. But for Americans, it is not even close to being true. America spends almost $8,500 per person a year on health care, which is as much as two or three times more than any other country. There are third-world countries like Cyprus, Slovenia, and Costa Rica that spend a fraction of what we do in America; their residents have less heart disease and live longer.

How can this possibly be true?

We are Americans. We live in the country where the motto is "Spend more; get better." If you spend more on a house, you expect to get a larger and better house. If you spend more on a car, you certainly expect a larger and better car. But when it comes to our health care, we are not getting what we pay for. In fact, we are getting ripped off.

This is the American paradox. We spend more on health care than other countries, yet it has not shown to pay off for our citizens. We spend luxury, sports car money, but only get the broken-down car that is on the side of the road with the white shirt hanging from the window and the hood opened up—the universal signal of "Help! I am broken down."

When I speak to groups or organizations, I will often raise the question as to why the audience thinks this is. That there is no money in helping people to be healthy is given as a reason almost every time. I think this statement is wrong, and the idea makes my skin crawl. Wanting people to be chronically sick so a company can sell its product to them is loathsome. Allowing a continuous flow of intentionally misguided information about what it means to be healthy and not just "not sick" is costly in not only dollars but lives, too. We have a government that has written innumerable pages on who will pay for health care but nothing on Americans being healthy.

These contradictions are the American paradox.

*Chapter 2*

# WE USED TO BE A WORLD POWER

Having the most weapons doesn't make us a world power. A world power leads. It leads other nations by showing them how great it is and how great other countries can be. We have exported democracy around the world, but we have also exported the American lifestyle and the state of American health. "Be like us. See how great we have it!" Countries and their citizens all over the globe still want a piece of the American dream.

Take, for example, the health of the second or third generation of immigrants who come to America. Unlike their parents, who hold on to their traditional customs and habits, the kids become Americanized[1,2,3]. The children eat and behave like American kids. They adopt American kids' health habits also. Although the kids might make fun of their parents for not eating the double-cheese-and-bacon-triple-bypass burger, the parents are healthier for it. The second generation will have the same cardiovascular issues as most Americans, while their parents, the first generation, will not.

If we truly want to be a world power again, we need to be a leader in health. We can lower our overall national spending on health care by billions each year, and then take that money and build an even better America, with better schools and playgrounds as the first step. For a country like ours that spends more than any other on a health care system that is not actually *health* care, you would think we would get better results for the money invested. But we don't. The product, our health, lags behind that of other countries, mainly because of both a pharmaceutical approach to nearly every symptom or disease, and a lack of progressive thinking about health among our leaders in government. I will discuss in the next chapter how our insurance companies could be the saviors of our country, but allowing them to dictate our health care would be ridiculous. Once again, if we want a healthier America, we need to have healthier Americans.

If a country really wanted to take over the United States, they could simply wait until we can no longer afford to maintain our defense budget because we are spending more and more money on keeping ourselves ill. With our poor overall health, a foreign country could cross our borders unopposed; we would not be well enough to do anything about it. Then again, *that* country would be saddled with taking care of us, and I do not think any country wants to take on that responsibility. Perhaps being this unhealthy is our best defense.

*Chapter 3*

# THE FALLACY OF UNIVERSAL HEALTH CARE

Health care was a hot topic in the 2012 presidential election the outcome of which could have immense ramifications for years to come. The major issue in America's health care debate is the idea of universal health care (UHC). The World Health Organization (WHO) defines UHC as "a system that ensures that all people have access to needed proactive, preventive, curative, and rehabilitative health services of sufficient quality to be effective, while also ensuring that the use of these services does not expose the user to financial hardship[4]."

While the primary advantages of such a system is that it can save lives, it also comes with significant costs. People die in our country each day because they cannot afford health care, but the WHO's definition of UHC leads to the following questions: How will we address the financial hardships of the employers and of the government that are expected to provide coverage in a universal system? Where does common sense and self-responsibility enter the equation? And what about the unintended consequences of a system that adds so many people in such a short period of time like the overcrowding of waiting rooms, shorter appointment times with the doctor, and even longer amount of days before getting into the doctor's office.

As employers pay more and more in health care costs for their employees, the number of employers who provide health care benefits declines. That said, it comes as no surprise that the costs of health care have increased in step with the decline of American health.

There are approximately anywhere from 49 million to 60 million Americans who are without health insurance, most of who are children. According to the CDC, more than one-third (35.7 percent) of all Americans are obese. Many suggest that the solution is universal health care, but is it?

The facts are plain and simple. Health care costs are greater now than ever before, and there are 49 million Americans, or approximately 16 percent of the US population, who do not have coverage. I believe everyone should have access to some form of health care, or at least emergency care, without having to worry about going bankrupt. But how do we go about doing that in a practical and productive manner?

Our health care system is very expensive and does not really address health at all; it addresses sickness and disease in a reactionary manner. In fact, according to recent statistics, we spend 2.5 times more per person on health care than any other Organisation for Economic Cooperation and Development (OECD) country in the world.

Let's address two main issues—the high cost of care and the high number, 49 million, of uninsured Americans. Some of our leaders have come up with the idea that America should follow the rest of the Western world by creating a universal health care system. But there are serious problems with the idea of universal health care in the United States.

Who will finance nationwide universal health care? I'm not just talking about the 49 million uninsured; I'm talking about all 311 million of us! A short time ago, our elected officials passed a Medicare prescription drug benefit (Medicare Part D) that we cannot afford. The Medicare prescription drug benefit is insurance that helps people pay for prescription drugs at participating pharmacies and is available to everyone who has Medicare. It provides protection if you pay high drug costs or have unexpected prescription drug bills. It does not cover all costs, however. You the patient ends up paying part of the cost of prescription drugs, and most people wind up paying a monthly premium as well as an annual deductible for the coverage. In a way, we end up paying three times for something that is sold to us as part of Medicare.

I am skeptical about anything that adds onto or extends from Medicare. Again, who is going to pay for it and how many times? Our government? We are borrowing money as a nation to pay for the wars we wage, and we want to add billions more a year for health care. Our nation simply cannot pay without significantly raising taxes. As I see it, there would have to be a large tax increase on all of us to make universal health care come close to being plausible. In a sense, it is like a dog chasing its own tail; if universal health care is implemented, we will be faced with the same problems we are facing now. We will likely continue to saddle employers with the cost of insuring employees and their families. Can the employer fire an employee for smoking, high blood pressure, high cholesterol, or a high body mass index, knowing that these are risk indicators for higher health care costs?

So you don't want to pay for it, the employers don't want to pay for it, and we sure as heck don't want higher taxes. But we are expected to head blindly into a Medicare-for-all type of system. The small matter of financing such a plan might need to be addressed fully and soundly before we even attempt to implement universal health care. Not only do our presidential hopefuls and governmental leaders need to hash this out, but they also need to explain it to us in simple terms. Here are the questions I would ask: What do we get and how much does that cost? For the 49 million Americans who do not have coverage, welcome to the game, you are now allowed to make co-payments.

One negative side effect to providing universal health care is what I call the "tuna can effect." Take for example a simple trip to the grocery store. If you were to buy just one can of tuna fish, it would cost $1.29. However, when the grocery store buys tuna, it buys in bulk, and therefore gets that same can for less at wholesale; that is the more cans of Tuna purchased, the better deal the grocery store gets. If 10,000 people buy cans of tuna, then the cost-per-can would inevitably decrease. But is the tuna any better? Or have we gotten the cheapest stuff possible?

Just as in the tuna can effect, when it comes to health care, I believe that operating on too large of a scale and consequently spreading something too thin causes it to lose its value. If we try to spread out our health care for the largest number of people, isn't it possible that the quality of care will deteriorate? After all, unlike tuna, the hospitals and doctors' offices will have more patients to deal with. This leads to another disadvantage: 49 million more Americans seeking health care services naturally results in a diminished availability of care. This will then create an unintended side effect of a system that intends to increase access, but instead decreases it and jeopardizes its quality. Picture waiting lists that could prevent people from getting the care they need. Now picture yourself on that waiting list.

So the answer to the who-will-pay-for-it question may be "all of us," through increased taxes and diminished quality of care. But another question still remains:

Are we going to be healthier?

The US health care system thrives on reactive responses to repair problems rather than taking a less exciting but far more effective proactive approach, which would avoid the problem altogether and reduce the need to have to react with expensive procedures and medications. For instance, we here in the United States are terrible at preventing heart problems, but we excel at doing double bypass operations with high survival rates. Likewise, we can't seem to get a handle on our cholesterol epidemic, but we certainly have an abundance of drugs to manage cholesterol. What does it say about a country that does a good job at doing a quadruple bypass and dolling out cholesterol drugs, but has little to no commitment to preventing the problems in the first place?

This one little dilemma seems to escape the pages and pages of statements about universal health care by our elected officials and in our mainstream media. It is a simple question: will these changes make us healthier?

Although being healthier is the underlying intention of all health care, no one actually talks about it. And no one says that we will be healthier for switching to a universal health care program. We will have new governmental agencies to ensure that doctors and hospitals are implementing "best practices," which, for you and me, means that someone somewhere did a study to find out how a doctor or hospital can provide the least amount of care and still get a certain outcome. This pushes individual care right out the door. And once again, it never comes close to helping you be healthier.

The new system, like our current one, will still be a reactive, "sickness care" system unless we make drastic changes in our health-care philosophy. If you put a bulldog in a tuxedo, do you know what you have? You have a bulldog in a tuxedo. (And they drool...a lot.) The same can be said of reactive health care—we can dress up the status quo in any outfit or ensemble we like, but if the only time people are allowed to go to a doctor or hospital is when they have something wrong with them, then we still have a reactionary system. Dress it up any way you want—it is still sick care (drooling in a tuxedo). We have yet to see anyone stand up and give us a plan that will not only reduce health care costs, but also help us be healthier.

There should certainly be a "sick care" safety net, in the case of major surgeries, accidents, and life-saving procedures. For a minimal amount, each person, or as many as can afford it, should pay for those who do not have any sick-care coverage, so at least these people do not have to mortgage their houses when someone in their family becomes ill. But this would still be sick care. When are we going to have a plan that aims higher? When will we have a directive that actually tries to make us healthier—not just symptom free? Not only do I think we *should* have this better plan, but it is absolutely necessary.

If we truly want to decrease health care costs, we need to decrease the consumption of health care. How much money does a healthy person consume in health-care dollars as opposed to a chronically ill person? Our focus should not be on the treatment of diseases—there will always be someone who has a disease—nor should it depend solely on the prevention of disease.

What we need to do is focus on helping people be healthier. If we want a healthier America, we need healthier Americans. And, as far as I know, there still is no pill or potion to take to be healthier. When all is said and done, it simply takes eating better, moving more, sleeping more than five hours a night, clearing the head of its daily jumble, and making sure our posture is proper.

The crazy part is that if we adopt a more preventative model, our insurance industry could come out as heroes. The insurance company calls you up (already unbelievable) and tells you that your premium for the upcoming year will be $1,000 (pretty good so far). They have already scheduled you for a battery of screenings and tests. You have an appointment with a trainer at the local gym to start your exercise program. Of course the gym would give a massive discount to insurance companies, as they will flood the gym with new members. You will exercise at a minimum of four times per week. I picture something along the lines of the Biggest Loser, minus all the pomp and circumstance of reality TV. You have already been set up with a nutritionist, dentist, chiropractor, primary care, etc. All this and your premium is only $1,000. If you choose not to take these health-promoting measures, then your premium will be $25,000 for the year. Which would you choose? Of course you would choose the first option. You spend a bunch less; you are (or become) a lot healthier; and the insurance company is now collecting premiums from healthy people and loving it.

If an ancient mystic or some sort of genie came to you and said that you have the opportunity to save a half a million dollars, just by being healthy, would you do it? Now pretend that genie is a health care insurance provider (okay, okay—perhaps it is a more realistic scenario when it is a genie). Nevertheless, for this to come true, we would all need to orient our philosophy toward a true health care (caring for health) system. We need to *universally* drop the ideas that support our reactionary sick care system. This is the sort of true *universal* health care I can get behind. This may be the biggest hurdle of any system that we adopt. We may all have a right to health care, but we also have a responsibility to be healthy.

What is perhaps most startling about the previous scenario, is that all of it could be undertaken right now.

*Chapter 4*

# THE PROFOUND LEAP FORWARD.

"The next major advance in the health of the
American people will be determined by what
the individual is willing to do for himself."
— John Knowles,
Former President of the Rockefeller Foundation

I am always in awe of people who think so far beyond the con-
text of their time that you have to stop and ask yourself, *How
did they get from here to there?*

The rock band Van Halen's first album came out when I
was in high school. Eddy Van Halen's guitar playing was light
years ahead of anyone else's at the time. Light years. He raised

the bar so high that the status quo became rubbish. All guitars have the potential to play the same notes, but Van Halen used this potential differently and expressed himself in a totally unique way. Jimi Hendrix must have had the same effect at his time. Guglielmo Marconi and the radio also come to mind when thinking about others who made profound leaps forward. Marconi decided to send invisible waves through the air so that people miles and miles away could hear them. Leonardo da Vinci drew submarines and flying machines. He was so far ahead that I wonder why he was not hunted down as a witch. The whole idea of the World Wide Web and all that can be done on computers mark an incredibly profound leap forward in how we process information.

We will see a profound leap forward in cars in the next five years as we go from a fossil-based fuel to alternative fuels.

We have seen profound leaps forward in the arts, philosophy, and science. One of my favorite websites is TED.com. TED stands for technology, entertainment, design. The organization holds a national conference once a year and brings leaders in these fields to present their current, cutting-edge research. Equally impressive is that each speaker must make his or her point in fewer than twenty minutes. The website is both terrifying and awe-inspiring!

But why hasn't there been a profound leap forward in the way we think about health care? I'm not referring to the technical aspects, like how we now use computer-guided therapies instead of manual ones, but rather the fact that these therapies still focus on relieving a symptoms or managing disease. The cable surgery channel demonstrates the incredible advances in life-saving techniques—infrared diagnostics, for example—but they are still premised on disease.

Hippocrates would spread mud on the back of his patients to see what area dried quicker, and from that he could determine that the nervous system was not working correctly in that area. He would follow that spinal segment's nerves to an organ to determine a disease process that may have been affecting it. I use a thermal scanning, computer-based system for the exact same reason. The tools are different, but the method of finding the information is the same. So now we can look into your body with a number of different tools like MRI (magnetic resonance imaging) techniques and CT (computed tomography)scans, while years ago we really only had x-rays. Before that, we had to actually look in the body through surgery to see what was going on.

When I read the latest research, it seems to be on such a minute level that the advance in knowledge from that research pushes the bar only a smidge forward. Obviously, we need to walk one step at a time in order to travel a mile. But when grants for research are destined to be used to find out whether one atom or another is affected by a particular process or pathogen, we must return to a more fundamental question, "Did the person live?" But the research isn't going there. We are stuck in finding out the tiny stuff and have lost track of the question of overall health. Where is the profound philosophical leap forward in how we care for people?

I was on a conference call with David Fletcher, DC, some years ago and he posed a question that I now use almost every time I open a presentation or talk: Are you using health care to see how great you can be, or are you just managing your symptoms and trying to stay alive? Every audience member whom I have asked this question has agreed with the second part of the question—that they are simply trying to stay alive.

This is because that is the only option given to us. Our health care system is based on a person having a symptom. The system is based on people being sick, not healthy.

Consider the following scenario: A patient goes into his family doctor for an exam. A typical American male, he has high blood pressure and a cholesterol problem. The doctor suggests that he should go on medications to decrease those. The patient responds that he does not want to go on medication and would rather work to try and lower his blood pressure and cholesterol on his own. The doctor then says that if the patient cannot lower those numbers in six months, he will prescribe the medications. The patient agrees.

The big problem is with the system as this scene is played out every day, in every city across the country. We have a doctor who is educated to take care of symptoms, but what is his education in health? What is his education in nutrition and exercise? None. MD's are notoriously uneducated in these areas. This is not simply an opinion; take a look at any medical school's curriculum, and you simply won't find classes on wellness and nutrition. So the doctor does not refer the patient to a nutritionist or trainer and does not give the patient the necessary information to succeed. The patient leaves with the limited skills, habits and education that brought on the high blood pressure and cholesterol. Is there any wonder why the patient is back in six months, and the prescription is waiting for him? It is a sucker bet. To tell someone he or she needs to change a lifestyle, but not give them any help in doing so is absolutely ridiculous.

Dentists are the closest we have to actually providing a health care model. Getting us to brush twice a day has a positive, measurable effect on our oral health. And besides having better teeth, people who brush and floss on a daily basis are less likely to have heart disease.

## A Step Forward

I am not suggesting that there is a single, profound leap forward we can take, but there are some small steps forward that will make a huge difference in managing our health. Here are a couple of them:

1. We—you and me—need to take charge of our health. It is *our* health and *we* should be the ones in the director's chair with a supporting cast of people to help care for our health. We need to realize our health belongs to us, and that we are responsible for it—not the insurance company, not the doctor, and not your mother. Only you.

2. Our "sick-care" system needs a revamp to truly become a health care system. The focus should shift away from disease care and prevention to the promotion of health. We can focus on disease prevention and talk about all the gains we are making against any one disease, but lose the overall battle for health. What good is it if we can prevent prostate disease, but the person has cardiovascular disease, or vice versa? We can talk prevention all we want, but if we truly want prevention, then we need to become healthier overall and not just single out individual diseases. Nixon waged a war against cancer. Why didn't he wage a war for health?

So maybe the profound leap forward in health needs to start with a look backward to see how our ancestors lived without all of the diseases we have. They did not live as long as us because of other fundamental problems like sanitation, cleanliness, food preparation and storage, health knowledge, etc. We now have access to the tools of knowledge and technology, but most of us have not even come close to our potential for pushing the boundaries of health. A profound leap forward should incorporate a multicultural view into our way of managing our health. Why are Japanese women pushing the longevity bar to almost eighty-six years while African-American men make it only an average of seventy years? We all come from the same stock. And in America we should be both ashamed and amazed that we are not the leaders in health. Good health is easy. Good health is natural. Healthy is the way we were born to be.

The profound leap forward needs to start with small steps to make huge gains for ourselves. Only we can do it. But the great thing is that we *can* do it.

Start with chapter 6, "The Healthy Eleven."

(See the chapters following the Healthy Eleven.)

Start by deciding which ones you are great at and which ones you need help in. Make a plan of attack and move forward.

So maybe this is where the leap starts, with a new idea for the plan on health. Let's wage our own war for health.

We need that profound leap forward in our health—and not just on the technological side, but on the interpersonal side. We need that leap forward on the you-and-me side. Some simple steps forward can lead to a profound leap.

Let's take it.

# Chapter 5

# PUTTING YOUR HEALTH ON THE BACK BURNER

I have patients who very obviously do not make their health a priority. It is not even that they put it on the back burner; they don't even get it on the stove! Actually they put it underneath the stove in the little pan drawer so they know where it is at just in case they need it, but out of sight enough so they don't have to be reminded every day.

The big problem with putting so little priority on health is that it will come back to bite you. Men are much more notorious for this than women. But with equal rights women are trying to be as stupid as men and not pay enough attention to their health. According to the Centers for Disease Control and

Prevention approximately 307,000 men die of cardiovascular disease a year equating to 1 in 4 men[5]. And although heart disease has traditionally be seen as a 'man's' disease, it takes the life of 292,000 women equating to 1in 4 women[6].

A buddy of mine who does very well for himself serves as the classic example. He is married with a couple of kids, and he is obviously not healthy. I was talking with him one day about a patient of mine who was not even close to being healthy. This patient had to work, work, work to make money, so his family could have a certain lifestyle. (Believe me, I am *all* for people having the lifestyle they want and making loads of cash, but not at the cost of their health?). The problem is that this particular patient was not taking care of himself. He frankly told me that he was going to make a lot of money now, and that he would take care of his health when he retired. I told the patient that he would burn through that cash that he had worked so hard for so quickly when he retired that his head would spin. And then what? Then he would have no cash and bad health. That equals *big*, expensive problems. I just didn't understand how anyone could think like that.

After I described this patient to my buddy on the phone, there was a long pause before my friend said "Screw you." I asked what *that* response was for? He replied, "You're talking about me." I had no idea but I *was* talking about him. I had not done so intentionally, but the shoe fit perfectly.

It is easy to take our health for granted because we have been lulled into the idea that if the smoke detector is not going off, there must not be a fire.

The number one reason for bankruptcy in America right now is health-care costs. This is even the case for people who *do* have insurance. Do you still need another reason to focus on your health?

I joined a business referral club, and I was speaking with a woman who worked for a national investment company. I told her about high bankruptcy rates due to health care costs, and she said "that is why I always recommend long-term health coverage for my seniors, so in case they have to go into a nursing home." I said I thought that type of coverage was good, but asked her why she didn't recommend "long-term health" instead? Instead of investing in coverage that is essentially premised on being unhealthy, why not invest in yourself to be healthy? Further, if you took all the money you were going to put into insurance and actually invested it in even something minimally progressive, you would have more than enough money to cover yourself if you needed to. But your health is not one dimensional; it has numerous advantages, like the potential to decrease overall health-care costs and to keep you independent longer. No insurance coverage can do that. I am not against long-term coverage by any means. But when the actuaries see that more and more Americans need long term care, it is because those people, our parents *(the Greatest generation)*, didn't have the health initiative like the next generation of Americans—the Baby Boomers. I can only hope that more Boomers take such good care of themselves that they never need long term insurance.

Your health is your wealth. If you want to retire wealthy, then you *must* retire healthy. Make your biggest investment in your own health. Who cares what car you own if you are not healthy enough to drive it.

Investing in your health pays massive dividends for life. This investment would be your "life insurance."

# Chapter 6

# THE HEALTHY ELEVEN

Often when I am at a health fair or at a posture screening, people will tell me "I don't need a Chiropractor, I already exercise." This is like saying, "I don't need a Chiropractor; I already brush my teeth." Exercising does not relate to how your nervous system is working. But to really get the person thinking, I love to say, "That is great. Are you doing the other ten things on the Healthy Eleven list?" The surprised look on their face tells me right away that they are not and that they have no idea what I am talking about.

There are at least eleven steps you should be taking every day to be your healthiest:

1.  Motion—you have *got* to move and keep moving.

2.  Fuel—you no longer think about what you eat as food, but *fuel*.

3.  Posture—a flat tire doesn't roll well, nor do people stay well with poor posture. Your Mom was right about the importance of posture!

4.  Rest—to be your best, you *must* get enough rest and it must be high quality. Napping is okay.

5.  Love—of course.

6.  Laughter—it decreases blood pressure, relaxes tight muscles, improves your immune system, and helps you live longer. Don't have anything to laugh about? Then look at yourself and don't take life so damn seriously!

7.  Friends—you are going to need help to be healthy when you are ninety-six and friends can help get you there.

8.  Vision/Goal/Intent for health—you either intend to be healthier or you do not; you cannot become healthy without that intention.

9.  Passion—everyone needs a reason to get up each morning. For some it might be a job, while for others it might be getting to do what they love. Either way, you must find a passion to add that juice to life.

10. Mental Stimulation—whether through a conversation over coffee with a colleague, a new class, the daily crossword, or a new hobby, pushing the connections in your brain on a daily basis makes you healthier.

11. PMA – Positive Mental Attitude (PMA)—everything is easier when the sun is shining.

How many steps of the Healthy Eleven do you do? How many of these steps need to be added to your daily health regimen? Once again, most of these come at little to no cost but can add life to your life and more life to your life.

*Chapter 7*

# MOTION

To reach your best health, it is absolutely mandatory that you move and that you move daily. Do something. Just get moving. If being sedentary was actually counted in the statistics of top killers of Americans, it would rank as number one. The lack of exercise in America is appalling, and people know it. With a list of reasons of why people can't exercise growing longer by the second, it is getting more difficult to change the trend.

So where do we begin? We start with the 2008 federal guidelines that state how long and how much you should exercise. Here I show the guidelines for adults, but there are also recommendations for children and seniors. Federal guidelines recommend:

> Adults (aged 18–64) should do 2 hours and 30 minutes a week of moderate-intensity physical activity or 1 hour and 15 minutes (75 minutes) a week of vigorous-intensity aerobic physical activity, or an equivalent combination of moderate- and vigorous-intensity aerobic physical activity. Aerobic activity should be performed in episodes of at least 10 minutes, preferably spread throughout the week.

> Additional health benefits are provided by increasing to 5 hours (300 minutes) a week of moderate-intensity aerobic physical activity, or 2 hours and 30 minutes a week of vigorous-intensity physical activity, or an equivalent combination of both.

> Adults should also do muscle-strengthening activities that involve all major muscle groups performed on 2 or more days per week.

The phrasing of and emphasis in those sentences is mine, but I want to make it obvious and apparent as to how much time you should be dedicating to your own health.

On the other hand, according to the A. C. Nielsen Co., the average American watches more than four hours of television each day (or twenty-eight hours per week, or two months of nonstop TV-watching each year). If you were to live to sixty-five, then you would spend about nine years just watching television. This breaks down to over 150 hours per month of watching the tube versus only ten hours of exercise!!!!

The following link from the CDC shows statistically what percentage of Americans is reaching those guideline goals. http://www.cdc.gov/nchs/data/hus/hus11.pdf#073

I have compressed the statistics below. What is apparent and scary is that the majority of Americans don't come close to reaching those guidelines.

| Age Group | Percentage who met recommended guidelines |
|---|---|
| 18–44 years | 25.7 |
| 8–24 years | 29.6 |
| 25–44 years | 24.3 |
| 45–64 years | 17.7 |
| 45–54 years | 19.2 |
| 55–64 years | 15.9 |
| 65–74 years | 13.6 |
| 75 years and over | 6.4 |

In my age group, 45–54 year olds, a scary 48.9 percent of respondents did not meet either the cardiovascular or weight bearing guidelines.

And here is where the road makes a big turn: when asking Americans if they exercise three or more times a week, nearly 52 percent of them responded affirmatively. The Gallup organization reports that there is a big discrepancy between the number of people who say they exercise three or more times per week versus the number who are actually reaching the federal guidelines for cardio and strength exercise. Gallup asked if the exercise was for "thirty minutes or more," not whether the respondent was walking, lifting weights, or running. Gallup only wanted to know that it was for thirty minutes or more. But even if thirty minutes of exercise was completed, it is still less than 50 percent of the federal guidelines even if we add a half an hour for each of the two days of weight lifting. So even the people who are doing what they think is the correct amount of exercise are falling very short of the recommended numbers.

Even more frightening is that nearly 30 percent of Americans do not exercise at all.

I am not sure where the idea of the thirty minutes, three-times-per-week plan came from, but it is now very common. As we see, however, it is not nearly enough. We need to get moving as a nation *much* more. Not moving is killing us.

This book doesn't feature photographs of models in work-out gear, demonstrating correct exercise poses and positions. There are many books that go into much more detail than I could give you here. What I am hoping for this book to do is to give you a big enough *WHY* you can be healthy and a new view that being healthy is innate without weighing you down with recipes and routines.

So we now know *how* much exercise should be included in our daily regimens. Now let's cement in the *why* of exercise. From the U.S. Department of Health and Human Services we see the benefits of physical activity[7]:

## Adults and Older Adults
Strong Evidence
- lower risk of
    early death

    heart disease (no need for the aspirin a day or those beta blockers)

    stroke (no need for the aspirin, cholesterol, or statin medications)

    Type 2 diabetes (no need for those sugar pills)

    high blood pressure (no need for the diuretics or beta blockers) adverse blood lipid profile (no need for the diuretics or cholesterol medications)

metabolic syndrome (no need for the cholesterol, sugar, diuretic medications)

colon and breast cancers (no need for surgery or chemo therapy)

- prevention of weight gain

- weight loss when combined with diet

- improved cardiorespiratory and muscular fitness

- prevention of falls

- reduced depression (no need for the antidepressant medications)

- better cognitive function in older adults, decrease dementia

## Moderate to Strong Evidence
- better functional health in older adults

- reduced abdominal obesity (no need for gastric bypass surgery)

## Moderate Evidence
- weight maintenance after weight loss

- lower risk of hip fracture (no need for calcium pills)

- increased bone density (no need for more calcium pills)

- improved sleep quality (no need for sleeping pills)

- lower risk of lung and endometrial cancers

## Children and Adolescents
Strong Evidence

- improved cardiorespiratory endurance and muscular fitness

- favorable body composition

- improved bone health

- improved cardiovascular and metabolic health biomarkers

Moderate Evidence

- reduced symptoms of anxiety and depression

Look at the list of the medications that could potentially be eliminated by exercise alone! It is staggering, isn't it? When a person is diagnosed with one of the conditions on the list above, why isn't the first thing that is prescribed a daily workout plan? It seems like that would have a positive impact on our country's major (and most expensive) illnesses. It would also decrease the amount of secondary drugs that are prescribed to take care of primary-drug side effects.

If you take *any* medications from the classes of drugs mentioned above, then it is especially important that you get moving. Do you need help getting started? Then get it! Would you like to get off those medications? Then get moving!

## Moving Your Spine

Yet another reason to have your spine adjusted by a chiropractor is to make sure it keeps moving—not just moving in the bend this way and that, but segmentally as well. Keeping those segments mobile helps keep your spine young. When your spine loses its proper motion or alignment, it can affect how your nervous system works. Just like with your body or your brain, not keeping motion in your spine allows it to grow old faster. Keep it moving!

Do you get the idea? Keep moving daily. Make a plan and a commitment to keep moving. I have my patients block out time in their weekly schedules for exercise and make that a priority. Everything else, besides family time and work, is scheduled around exercise because it is *that* important.

*Chapter 8*

# FUEL AND FOOD

How many diets have you been on? How many new meal plans have you seen on the morning shows that made you think *Now* this *is what I need to help me lose those pounds and get back into shape!* You dedicate a strong, two or three weeks to this newest, greatest plan. You go to the grocery store and get all the food the new great diet requires. You find that one super-secret supplement that will melt away the pounds. Your mind was made up that *this* would be just what you need.

And then just one weekend and you are back to the same unhealthy American diet that is slowly robbing you of health.

How did you fall so quickly back into the same exact rut? Did you all of the sudden lose the information you had gained just a few weeks prior about that great new diet plan? No. Did you misplace the paper on which you wrote the plan? No. Then what is the difference?

## Why Do We Make Eating So Difficult

In America we have new diet books on a regular basis that we think will save us, and each book is outdone by the next. When did we get so far away from simple, healthy eating?

So I am going to proclaim the next great diet is to eat healthy.

Start with fresh fruits and vegetables. I know that this is not nearly as exciting as joining a plan that sends pre-packaged foods to your house. But you also never learn how to be a healthy eater on those plans. You learn to eat that company's foods. For some people this may be a jumping off point to then find the foods they need. But for most it is just another eating plan that they take on, follow, and abandon whenever the desired effect has been achieved. If there is no basic informational platform that allows you to know why this food is healthier than that, you will never progress.

## Simple Eating Rules

1. **Eat Fresh Fruit and Veggies**

2. **If it can sit on your shelf for more than a couple of days without spoiling, don't eat it.**

This one will kill most people. I hear, "But I love …" so often. I know you love your favorite foods that are slowly killing you, mostly because of the soft addictions of sugar, salt or fat that goes along with them. Listen, I am a sugar guy. My tiramisu and I have a personal relationship, but I do not eat it at home.

For me, this approach works. When I go do to dinner, I will order desserts, but since I do the majority of the grocery shopping, I simply choose not to buy them. If the food that you love can sit on your shelf for more than a week without spoilage, then imagine what is in it that allows it to be that way. *Then* imagine what it is doing to you and your kids.

### 3.   If you don't buy it, you won't eat it.

It doesn't get much simpler than this. If it is not in the shopping cart, then it won't be in the house. Don't even put unhealthy items on the shopping list. Again, I get it. I could *easily* eat a half-gallon of ice cream in a couple of days—no problem. The justification would be that it is just one, simple treat to myself. I have been there and done that many times. I still struggle with this issue on a weekly, if not daily, basis. But I simply do not buy it. I have my list, and I stick to it. "But I like," "my kids really like," or "my husband really likes …" doesn't factor into my grocery shopping. Those sentences never seem to end with "broccoli" or "spinach salad"; but they always end with something artificial—extra sugar, crunchies, dyes, colorings, or artificial flavors. These foods can sit on the shelf for decades and will undoubtedly be packaged with nutritional information highlighted and some other form of "natural" rhetoric. That company has spent many, many hours working on that package, so you will buy it. They have manipulated the taste, texture, and smell in a lab somewhere so that you will crave it again and again.

### 4.   If you would not feed it to your dog, don't eat it.

It is amazing how we allow ourselves to devour foods that we consider okay for us, but we wouldn't give them to the dog. Have you ever seen your dog sit down to a big bowl of chips on a Saturday night? Would you even think of giving them to him? You might sneak him one until your spouse catches you and gives you the stink eye and says, "I am *not* cleaning *that* up!" (I've been there, too!) We want our cherished pets and best four-legged friends to be around as long as possible and as healthy as they can be during that time. We do not give them the same sort of "treats" we give our kids.

## 5.  Do *not* use the word "treat" when giving candy or fast food to your kids.

This language sets up a whole neurological cascade in their bodies, which once started is tough to stop. You have taught them that if they behave, you will reward them with candy or fast food—frankly the worst stuff on earth to use as a reward. Sugar and fast food change them chemically. I have had parents in my office who say similar things to their kids, "if you are quiet I will give you this bag of multi-colored, dyed, hyper-sugared candies that will have you bouncing off the walls in no time, and I will wonder why you won't eat dinner." Don't start that whole association with your kids. When the positive association with junk food is started as a kid, it follows into adulthood and is difficult to break.

## 6.  Great taste, texture, and smell beat sheer volume every day.

If you want to make a change in your diet, use more spices, herbs, tastes, aromas, etc. When my wife and I were in Italy, we ate five-course meals every night. The sensation overload was magnificent. Not once did we come away from what we Americans would consider eating marathons feeling the full-bellied sluggishness that we regularly have here. Instead, we had five-course meals that were full of incredible aromas, colors, textures, and tastes—oh, the tastes. We were not sure what we were eating all the time, but we were sure that it was great.

It seems in America that we have traded those exceptional eating experiences for quantity. You will either be satisfied by tastes, smells, and textures or by belly fullness. I have no doubt that while we were in Italy our senses said "enough," while our bellies said "still have room." In America it seems to be the opposite in that our bellies say, "enough," while our senses have not been tempted nearly enough.

I have had to learn how to cook. Make no mistake; I am no magician in the kitchen by any means. My brother Rick is a chef who takes three ingredients and half a chicken and makes a wonderful dinner. He is a regular MacGyver of the cutting board. I have no such talent. I can read a recipe eight times and still cannot convert cups to quarts or pounds to whatever they need to be. But I have discovered that the rest of the world and our ancestors used all types of flavors in their foods that we have gotten away from in our modern times. Ginger, pepper, and basil are just a few of the great tastes I love. Discover your own. Experiment. Take a drive to a new type of restaurant or get an easy cookbook. You will be amazed at how simple some recipes are, and how delicious they can be.

## 7.  Carbohydrates are neither good nor bad.

You need carbohydrates in your diet on a daily basis. If you were to cut out carbs from your diet you would miss out on some of the most beautiful of fruits and vegetables on the earth. There are no good carbs or bad carbs. There are foods that will either promote health, or not. You cannot compare a head of broccoli to a cupcake. Both are carbs. One kills cancer; one doesn't. What is funny about the whole carb debate is that no one talks about good and bad fats or good and bad protein. We can make choices from the best of each group and make incredible meals out of all of it and still have great taste while also promoting health and decreasing inflammation.

I hear people say that they are cutting out carbs. It can't be done—not in a healthy meal plan, that is. It is easy to cut out sweets, but those aren't just carbs. There are also a load of fat and sugar in those sweets.

So it is not the carbs alone that are damaging to us. It is the choice of carbs we make. We must make better choices in what we eat. When in doubt, ask yourself, *Will this make me healthier?* or *Will this promote my healing?*

I enjoy food as much as anyone else. As I have told many people, tiramisu and I have an understanding. I will drive for tiramisu. Although it is my favorite dessert, I don't have it often—maybe a few times a year at most. If I did have it more often, I would have to find a tailor to let out all of my trousers. I understand this is not something that will let me reach my health goals and can easily set me back. So I don't have it.

It is actually easier to make a good choice when eating than to have to work on the consequences of a bad one.

To make it even easier for you, try to follow some easy ideas about your fuel:

Food should really come down to four requirements. It should be:
1. Nutritious;
2. Easy to make or eat;
3. Appetizing and appealing to all the senses;
4. Plentiful or at least easily accessible.

*Chapter 9*

# YOUR MOM WAS RIGHT ABOUT POSTURE

Your mom *was* right about posture—stand up straight and stop slouching!

Being built correctly directly determines how well you can physically function. In other words, can a tire that should have thirty pounds of air pressure in it, but only has twenty-five, work at its best? No way. You can still drive the car, but the brakes won't work as well, the brakes will take longer to work, the steering won't be as easy, and the alignment will be off. You will burn more gas and oil just because you have a tire that is not fully inflated.

The same is true with your posture. Sure, you can still stand up and do the things you want, but can you do them as well or as long as you want?

Recent research shows that seniors who have a head-forward posture (you see these people every day—the head way forward of their trunk) have advanced atherosclerosis[8]. In English: the seniors who have the head forward posture have advanced hardening of the arteries and other organs. The study shows that persons who have even a slight head-forward position (hyperkyphosis or too much curve in the back) had a 1.44 times greater mortality rate and had an increased rate of atherosclerosis of 2.4 times. Regardless of exercise, nutrition or supplementation these seniors are growing older from the inside out!

When your posture is not correct, it causes stress on your nervous system and spine. With the head-forward posture, your neck will decay and grow older much quicker. This decay is visible in the spine as spurs on some, but not all, of the vertebrae. If there were normal decay, all of the bones in your spine would show the same rate of deterioration. With abnormal postures, the spine frequently shows regions with advanced decay that is not visible in other areas. This is not normal aging. This is the result of stress being put on particular areas of the spine, which show those stresses in the advanced decay.

In my office we call it the "secretary posture," the "student posture," or the "teacher posture," as all of these people typically sit for long periods of time and either look forward or down. With the mass use of computers we can add "computer posture" to the list, as well.

I have been asked to perform the scoliosis (curvature of the spine) checks in elementary schools numerous times. What I see more often than scoliosis is the head-forward position. The American Academy of Orthopedic Surgeons state that "scoliosis curves measuring at least 10 degrees occur in 1.5 percent to 3.0 percent of the population." Griegel-Morris, et al, state that the head forward posture may be seen in over 66 percent of the population[9].

One of the simplest exams to administer and to undergo and that gives an invaluable amount of information is a posture exam. We do our posture exams using an iPad; but a keen eye and knowledge of what to look for is all that is really needed.

Correcting posture takes time; people who enter our office have usually had this posture for years, if not decades. But correction of the posture can be done and can have incredible benefits to your overall health. Get your posture checked.

*Chapter 10*

# REST

When we are hungry, we eat. When we are thirsty, we drink. When need to go to the bathroom, we go. When we are tired, we drink a super energy drink. How did this fundamental part of addressing our needs get so messed up?

When we were children, our parents knew right away when we needed to take a nap or go to bed. As adults ourselves, we seem to have forgotten how to do this. We think that if we just can stay up a little longer finishing the project it will be okay, even though we can barely keep our eyes open, and our minds cannot focus. So go to bed already!

When a person starts care in my office, I don't look for their initial complaint of a symptom to decrease as the first sign that he or she is getting better. The first sign I look for is when he or she says, "I think I am sleeping better." When we sleep, we repair our bodies from all the stuff we do during the day that breaks us down. It might be the food we have eaten, the sitting in front of the computer for all those hours, the repetitive lifting, or the stresses of deadlines; all of these stressors cause us to break down a little each day. When we get good sleep, we can repair the damage. If we do not get good sleep—whether in quantity or quality—we don't repair. The body has its own, incredible reboot and repair mechanism, just like a computer. Your computer reboots and repairs when it is not doing big work during the day. Your computer reboots and repairs when you are asleep. Your body does the same. For your body to reboot and repair, which allows your immune system to work at its best, you must have both good quality and a good quantity of rest. The appropriate amount is different for each person, but each individual knows what is appropriate for him or her.

So plan on getting the sleep you need nightly. You can't just make it up on the weekends. If you need a full eight hours, then plan on getting ready for and into bed early so you can get your necessary "reboot and repair" time. As with children, we help them unwind by getting ready with a bath and putting pajamas on at a certain time each night. You should do the same; have a nightly plan to get ready and then into bed for sleep.

What do Ronald Reagan, Albert Einstein, and Dr. B. J. Palmer have in common? They all took naps. It is okay to nap. A quick fifteen- to twenty-minute nap can do an incredible job of recharging your batteries and helping you focus on the rest of the day. This does not mean taking a two-hour sleep bomb, as that would wreck your sleep that night. Many cultures make napping part of their normal day. In America we see it as a sign of weakness. Think about your baby again. It is mandatory that they take an afternoon nap, and we all know what happens if the baby doesn't get his or her nap! It's okay to nap. Take the time to recharge. You will like it, and you will benefit from it.

*Chapter 11*

# LOVE

An essential ingredient for a healthy life is love. Many books and articles have been published showing that married people live longer than single people. The love need not be that all-consuming, fire-raging, toe-tingling, we-can-love-each-other-with-no-money,-food,-or-shelter, against-all-odds kind of love you see on the movie screen, although that would be fantastic. Yes, it may be *the* most difficult of all the ingredients in this book to manage, as it takes two people to really make it. But once attained, there is no denying that when love is great, it is stellar.

An incredible product of love is often children. Who doesn't love kids? If there were an all-time list of the greatest sounds on earth *ever,* children laughing, in any language, must be at the top. And most of the time the kids come about from a couple who is in love. And yes, I count gay couples among them.

Two dreamy eyed teenagers looking deeply into each other's souls say simultaneously, "Let's grow old together." This doesn't happen unless you are healthy. As a baby boomer watching my parents grow old and my Mom slowly decline from pulmonary fibrosis, I try to be healthy so I can take care of my wife if needed or so she doesn't have to take care of me. (See the conclusion of the book for more on this topic.)

For your best health, there needs to be a variety of kinds of love. Loving yourself and who you are is a key component of your health. How could you reach your best health if you didn't really like yourself? It has nothing to do with being a braggart or showing the world how great you are. It has everything to do with looking out for yourself and making the best decisions for yourself. Over the decades I have seen many people in my chiropractic office who are committed to fitness, exercise on a regular schedule, eat smartly, get chiropractic adjustments on a regular basis, and look good physically. But a key lynch pin to good health was missing; they weren't able to say that they liked themselves. There have even been some people who did not feel they were worthy of good health. The mountain they have to climb to be healthy is extremely steep, though it is not impossible to scale.

We must love life itself; love the idea of spending time with people; and love watching "how the kids have grown." We must love the juice that comes from giving that extra ounce of sweat and knowing it made all the difference. We must want to  share life with the world and take the steps daily to make it all happen again tomorrow. You have to squeeze the other person so tight during a hug that you are not sure that your cells haven't undergone some sort of love osmosis. It warms me to hear friends say that life is good with little twinkles in their eyes and sly smiles on their faces; they are showing that life is a little more than good—that life is great, and they are loving it.

It would be wonderful if everyone could love their occupations and get paid well to do them. Many people have jobs. Some people are lucky enough to do something they deeply love and to pick up a pay check for it. These people do not go to work; they go to a calling. The people who have this type of job always seem to be happier at work; they seem to not get injured at work as often, and they seem to age slower than people who have, simply, jobs. We see people who age at a dramatic pace when they hold jobs they hate. I know that not everyone can have a calling that pays the mortgage, the car payment, and keeps food on the table. If this is you, then what do you love? What is your passion? If you could do anything and get paid for it, what would that be? So why not do that anyway? If you like doing that one thing—like painting, coaching, teaching a certain skill—that would make your life better and more enjoyable, then why not do that one thing anyway? If you really love doing that one thing, then you likely have a natural talent for it, and it probably comes very easy for you. So share the positive love vibrations with more people. With you taking up or getting back into a hobby that you love and that brings zest into your life, then you should take immediate action to get back to doing that. If it is a hobby, then call it a hobby. Everyone should have one that they love. Many people have a hobby that they love, which allows them to keep returning to the job that pays the bills. It is a necessary trade off. The critical point is to find that *one* thing. Stay your healthiest so you can make a difference in someone else's life.

Do you have friends in your life who you just *love*? I am not referring to drive-by acquaintances, but deep friendships.

I mean the friends who you may see only once a year, and it seems like you saw each other yesterday? *That* kind of love is essential. Friends like that don't just fall from the coconut tree every day, and when you are with them, you are both better for your time together; you both consider those times special. Stay your healthiest so you can enjoy them.

How many of you could live without music? I *love* music. I am a mediocre musician and an even worse singer. Neither one of these facts has stopped me from singing in the shower, my car, my office, or anywhere else. Music has the incredible ability to take you back to your first kiss, your seventh grade dance, your college years, and even to tragic events. But I still love music. If you are like me, you could not imagine a day without music. What else is in your life that you could not imagine even a day without? As long as it is not detrimental to your family or your health, you should dive deeper into it. Stay healthy so you can listen, and rock, a little more.

These are a few of the key loves that you can and will experience in life. To a very powerful extent, your health determines how much you will love. Be your healthiest so you *can* love longer and more. And I almost forgot to mention one of the richest loves of all: the love of the New York Yankees.

*Chapter 12*

# LAUGHTER

A terribly overlooked part of your health is the ability to laugh. As I mentioned in the last chapter, the sound of a child laughing may be a universally incredible and heartwarming sound. When you see a big smile on the face of a child and hear his or her belly laugh, you automatically respond with a smile and your own laughter. Pamela Gerloff, EdD, in her article, "Are You Meeting Your Laugh Quota? Why You Should Laugh Like a 5-Year-Old,"[10] showed that young kids laugh hundreds of times a day, while adults laugh fewer than ten times! Since when did we have to take things so seriously that we can't laugh? As adults have we taken ourselves so seriously that we can't even laugh at our own stupidity? By the way, we *are* stupid, as YouTube reminds us daily.

There are numerous health benefits from laughing, such as lowered blood pressure, a reduction of the stress hormones cortisol and adrenaline, and a good workout for your abdominal and facial muscles. A study at Johns Hopkins University[11] showed that having a good laugh during instruction can lead to better test scores. If you wanted to boost your immune system, you should laugh more as it helps to increase tumor-killing cells.

Yes, you can get a great abdominal workout by laughing. If the laughter is hearty enough, you might even empty your bladder just a little bit, but this chapter is not meant to bore you with all the scientific aspects of laughing. Just realize that there are not many things that can be so well shared between two people as a good, can't-catch-my-breath, talk-stopping, crying-for-minutes laugh.

An incredible health goal would be to laugh more every day.

And yes, I *do* think the sound of a child laughing is the greatest sound ever. The second best is the vast sound of nature that I was surrounded by at the North Rim of the Grand Canyon at Bright Angel Point. The third best must then be the sound of popcorn popping. First, you know what you are going to eat in just a few minutes. But it also means that it is movie night and you will be cozying yourself up on the couch in a blanket next to someone you love, and that is always good!

*Chapter 13*

# FRIENDS AND FAMILY

It is unimaginable for us to think that we might not have loved ones with us throughout our lives. Just as heartbreaking would be a life not lived with the help, love, talks, and laughs of friends.

People who belong to groups, whether a church, social club, or the regulars you see at the gym daily, have better health outlooks than those who do not socialize in groups. People who belong to groups live longer. Maybe they are driven by their desire to see other people and be socially active. Some of it may be the mental or physical stimulation that goes along with group interaction. Either way, having a group to belong to is essential for good health.

I have patients who have not seen certain family members for years. They have no idea what these people are doing, how they are doing, or exactly where they live. This is so unthinkable for me. It is not a matter of being on the phone every day with your family or friends, as the most comforting idea is that they are just there—only a phone call away. There are times when we don't see eye to eye with family members over something that has happened. It is not necessary for there to be total agreement on every single family issue for there to be love in a family.

I could go into any dozen of family issues that have arisen on the back porch of my Aunt Gen and Uncle Jim's house. This is a small back porch, which by state regulations should only hold about five or six people, but at our annual Fourth of July bocce tournament and parade (yes, we have a parade!) the back porch may hold well over a dozen crammed-in cousins who are carrying on in a number of discussions at once. It can get loud and sometimes heated with opinions flying from corner to corner about politics, religion, government, education, or even the treacherous subject of bocce tournament pairings. During election years the heat can get turned up even more. But at the end of the day, we have no doubt that there is love for everyone in that room no matter how different their opinion may be. We are family and always will be. We are allowed to voice our feelings without being scorned. It is that time on the back porch to which we all look forward and which we find hard to imagine not happening one day. Some newbies to the family are somewhat taken aback by our family's ability to debate strongly and wash it away at the end of the day. In our family, that *is* what it means to be family. If you are not able to take a hit and throw a couple, you may have your family ID card revoked.

We love talking about our family, our heritage, our parents, and grandparents, and we love learning more and more from our aunts and uncles about "us." The bond we have is unshakeable. We are family. (Cue song!)

You should also share the same type of bond with your dearest friends. How many times have you called your best friend and said, "Do you have a minute? I need to talk!" They listen quietly as you take over the conversation. When you are done they give their best help and give you a hug. That is what friends do. Whether your best grade school friend to your best new friend you met last year, all true friends have a piece of you in them and them in you. It is comforting to know they are there. My buddy, Franc, and I will recall with clarity events from decades ago and laugh hysterically. We don't have to talk every day, but I know deep down he is always there for me. That is what friends are for.

So you just can't go out and make a best friend. Just like the beautiful roses my dad grew, friendships take time to cultivate, but they are *so* worth it.

Having friends and family makes you healthier. Take the time to nurture those relationships.

*Chapter 14*

# YOUR VISION OF HEALTH

Do you see yourself as healthy?

The next four steps of the Healthy Eleven can *all* be introduced into your life with no money at all. These are by far the cheapest ways to get really healthy. They are also the most critical and usually the most overlooked and underutilized.

When asked what their health will be like in ten, twenty, or thirty years, many people look away, slump their head forward, roll their shoulders in, and give the international sign of giving up. They raise their head and say, "not so good, Doc." Where on earth did they get this idea that your health is automatically going to be worse with age? I will admit that the opportunity for disease is greater, but that is only because the older we get, the more opportunities we have to screw up our health. Sitting on the sidelines and being an innocent bystander to your health is no longer an option. You must be an active participant in your health. It is your boat, and you are the captain. Steer it to the lush, beautiful islands and calm waters of health.

But just like the captain of the boat, the potential for good health is determined by the map you have on board. Your map for health is your vision of what you will be like in the future. It does not matter how healthy your parents or siblings are; your health is determined by your own map. So get a *great* map.

"Vision" refers to the way you see your own health. Do you see yourself as healthy and vibrant in those ten, twenty, or thirty years, or do you see yourself as being dependent, immobile, and lacking the spark of life? How you see yourself determines the way you will act. Your vision of your personal health decades in the future will determine your actions and behavior today.

Can your health get drastically worse? Yes, and I see people taking those steps daily. Can your health get drastically better? Yes, and I see people taking those steps daily. The major difference is how individuals see themselves in the future. So start seeing yourself as someone who rocks and will keep rocking!

Goals are important in determining your vision of yourself. Is it your goal to be a healthy, vibrant, and independent person who contributes to society in their eighties and nineties? Or are you going to leave it up to the universe to decide what your health will be? Once you tell the universe that you have no goal for health, the universe will give you one, and it is never the one you would have chosen.

My goal is to be ninety-six and the all-time pitcher for our neighborhood kickball team. (Does anyone play kickball anymore?) My goal is to be active, involved, educated, and one damn sexy man well into my golden years.

What are your goals for health? For most people it is to lose a certain number of pounds in a few months. That is not truly a health goal, but rather one step toward a goal. Think bigger; think of the vibrant energy of living and loving well into the future and the opportunities that come with it.

When asked how old they expect to live, many people shoot so low it is sad: "Oh, about sixty-five or so." First, sixty-five is lower than the average age most Americans reach now, much less in the next decades. Second, when asked why that particular age, they typically respond that they saw the poor health of their parents, and they don't want to live like *that*. If you don't want to live like your parents, then you have two choices: have a much shorter life, or *change* the way you live and make it better.

Intent follows right along with having a goal of health. Intent, as described by the Merriam-Webster dictionary, is "the design or purpose to commit an act, the state of mind with which an act is done, usually clearly formulated or planned."

You can have a vision of health. You can have a detailed goal of health. But if your intention does not include taking those daily steps, then the first two steps of this Healthy Eleven are useless. You must take action for your health. Aiming to sit by and watch what happens is an intention, and you have taken action. Daily planning of the best fuel, exercise, rest, time with friends is an incredible statement about the importance of your life.

Your vision should be to see the healthiest you years and decades in the future.

Your goal should be the plan you have to reach that healthiest you.

Your intention is the mindset and action you take today to reach your healthiest you.

Make it your daily intention, your daily focus, your daily plan to become just a little bit better. It will make all the difference to the future you.

*Chapter 15*

# PASSION

What gets you up in the morning—besides the alarm clock?

A better question might be: what makes you *want* to get up in the morning? If we could all answer this question, we would all be much happier. The incredible sight of people working their fingers to the bone daily for a job they hate, only to go home, watch hours of mindless television, go to bed, and get up to do it all over again just for a paycheck makes me cringe. This is more like the un-American dream; this picture cannot be what our parents worked their backs to the bone for.

Among the thousands of people I have been lucky enough to meet in my office are many who work in jobs they hate.

Their jobs absolutely beat them up. Sometimes their jobs beat them up on the outside, but usually they are eaten up from the inside. They do it for what they consider to be good pay and benefits. There is no passion. There is no sparkle in their eyes. The light seems to have been snuffed out, and they don't know how to rekindle the fire. For them, life is a day-by-day existence with only distant hope of retirement.

There are those people we meet who are lucky enough to have a job that is really a passion for them. Their paycheck is tied to what they live for. I would have to imagine that this is a small percentage of people. Just ask your friends, or even your co-workers, how many of them actually love going to work and have a passion for what they do. Some will say that they love what they do, or love going to work, but few will say that they have a passion for their job. So what are you to do if you are not someone who is absolutely ablaze about your job?

Find a passion.

For the majority of people their passion lies outside the walls of the workplace. It might be the band you and your buddies play in. You and everyone who has heard your demo tapes knows that you are not going on tour anytime soon, but you *love* to play! With the onset of technology that allows someone like me, who is tone deaf, to record music in his den is like magic to me.

Some readers will undoubtedly work all forty hours in the week, just so you can take a couple of hours on your days off to get on your motorcycle and go for a ride. Many of you have told me that those few of hours of riding outweigh the forty of working. That is passion.

Your passion might be seeing your kids grow up into young adults, and this makes your heart race a little and puts a smile on your face. Your passion may not be the same when you are older and your kids have grown and moved out. You are allowed to have more than one passion in your life as you evolve and opportunities come up. Sometimes your job gives you the financial ease to enjoy your passion or enjoy your passion more.

Painting. Photography. Your favorite team. Reading.

What is *your* passion?

What would make you want to get out of bed a little earlier or go to bed a little later just to have more time to do? People who say they don't have a passion, simply haven't found that passion, yet; or worse, they are afraid to go get it. Having a passion will make the day go quicker, will make life a little tastier, and will make life a little easier.

*Chapter 16*

# MENTAL STIMULATION

Get your head moving.

A frequently overlooked area that also needs exercise is the six inches of gray matter between your ears—your brain. Just as important as keeping your body moving is to keep your brain moving, that is, to keep learning.

I was speaking in Mr. Jeremy Milligan's high school psychology class when a student asked about our how our brains learn in adulthood. The student was under the assumption that after a certain age—for that student, the old age was, say twenty-five or thirty!—our brains stop learning. I asked the student if she had grandparents, and she said yes. I then asked if there is there any technology that has come out in her lifetimes that was not available before she was born and to which her grandparents would not have had access. She again answered yes. "Then how did they learn to use that technology?" I asked. Our brains may stop growing in sheer size, but we never stop learning. The great Dr. Joe Dispenza, in one of his incredible presentations, shows live neurons connecting or pruning, depending on the action or thought of the patient. The stronger the thought or more the patient does the action, the stronger the neuron becomes. What is perhaps most incredible is that our brains create new neuron connections all the time. It has to; if it didn't, we would all die from some easily avoidable accident. No one would live past that ripe old age of twenty-five or thirty.

The great cellist Pablo Casales was asked why he still practiced for three hours a day even into his eighties. Casales replied, "I think I am getting better."

Your mind was meant to continue learning and growing throughout your life. We do get into lifestyle ruts like watching TV automatically after dinner, since we think we need to rest from our workday. That same time could be used studying or at the very least reading. For the most part, watching TV is non-thinking time. It takes no thought to watch—even if it's an educational program. It does take thought to read and comprehend new information, however. When people say that they do not have time to read, learn a new language, or even do the crossword, I ask them if they could manage to turn the television off for one hour a day. Imagine what could be learned, planned, or completed in that hour. I wrote this book by dedicating focused time to it; I even turned the TV off when the Yankees were on.

Would you rather have a healthy body and an ill mind or be lucid into your senior years and with a feeble body? I would prefer to have both and intend to. Most people would first choose the lucid mind. So get engaged and stretch yourself a little bit farther.

But how do you go about engaging yourself? It is easy and can cost little to nothing to do. Below is a list of a few of the possibilities of how to keep your mind young and active:

Read every day and in different genres. Learn an instrument. And another. Exercise daily. Learn a new word each day and have fun by telling your friends (and bugging them) about the word of the day. Take a class. Take a class online. Write with your non-dominant hand. Cook. Talk with your friends daily. Join Toastmasters. Volunteer. Write a book. Laugh. Laugh more. Write a thank you letter everyday to someone who touched you. Get artistic. Get scientific. Get healthy. Write your own biography. Make a contract with yourself to become an expert in a subject, any subject.

I am sure you could add dozens and dozens more activities to this list. Keep pushing a little more every day. With the anticipation of a generation of Alzheimer's-debilitated seniors, the Boomer generation is feeling a great need to delay and change that likelihood. Alzheimer's medications are not, yet, a viable option for prevention or treatment. We need to get Boomers healthier and keep them exercising their brains, *now*. You and I need to start now.

These small steps can have a profound effect on all of us, but we need to remember to exercise our brains as much as our bodies.

*Chapter 17*

# A POSITIVE MENTAL ATTITUDE

It is impossible to experience radiant sunshine everyday of your life. Even the most beautiful of flowers requires rain for growth. Flowers would die if all they received was continuous sunshine.

A positive mental attitude—or positive mental health—is not the absence of fear, but the confrontation of fear. We all have fears. You can be afraid and *still* take a step forward.

- It is not the absence of failure, but the ability to learn from your failures and still make forward progress.

- It is realizing your strengths and using those special talents to improve yourself, your community, and your world.

- It is accepting yourself for who you are and who you want to be and *still* taking a step forward.

- It is asking for help, accepting help, and asking how you can improve.

- It is not being afraid of your dreams, but realizing that dreams are meant to be envisioned in your mind, held in your heart, and worked through your hands.

- It is finding love in people, places, actions, and ideas.

- It is laughing every day—mostly at yourself.

- It is stretching and pushing yourself just to see how far you can go and realizing it wasn't that far at all.

- It is lending a hand to someone else.

- It is knowing that giving a hug is a great drug.

- It is knowing when to be strong, when to be vulnerable, when to be open, when to be quiet, and when to listen.

- It is knowing that it is acceptable to be magnificent in at least one thing in life.

- It is knowing that if you can make a child laugh, you have made the universe laugh also.

- It is loving, being loved, and loving to be loved.

- It is knowing that we already have all the tools needed to be great, that we may need to read the instruction manual, be we are fully equipped to be our best.

Having a positive mental attitude takes no money. You do not need a five-letter degree from a major university to have it. What is needed is to take one step forward in your dreams even in the face of fear or adversity.

You can do it if you believe.

# Chapter 18

# THE NEXT GREAT EPIDEMIC: HEALTH

The Merriam-Webster Online Dictionary defines epidemic as:

1. affecting or tending to affect a disproportionately large number of individuals within a population, community, or region at the same time <typhoid was *epidemic*>

2. a: excessively prevalent, b: contagious <*epidemic* laughter>

3. characterized by very widespread growth or extent: of, relating to, or constituting an epidemic <the practice had reached *epidemic* proportions>

America has been haunted by the ghost of the Great Flu Pandemic (an epidemic on many continents) of 1918 and has consequently anticipated many other similar epidemics like the swine flu or, more recently, the bird flu epidemics. Each one of the newer epidemics is predicted to be more devastating and deadly than the previous. Our government health agencies meet to anticipate closings, emergencies, and deaths. Millions upon millions of dollars are set aside for each of these illnesses with the anticipation of the worst outcome. Fear is always prevalent in the broadcasting of information about any epidemic and the dark shadow it will cast over our communities and lives.

Could we start a new epidemic? Instead of waiting for the next great plague to affect mankind, can't we systematically plan our next great epidemic to be one that sweeps our nation into greater health? Instead of using the millions of dollars in emergency resources to clean up the effects of a virus, could we be a nation that promotes the health of our citizens so we will be less susceptible to the next virus?

There will always be a next virus, but it doesn't have to be a killer. If we took a fraction of the money we use to in the planning for the epidemic illnesses and used it to push Americans toward greater health, we may actually lay a plan for preventing the next great epidemic.

Ironically, our National Institutes of Health (NIH) are much more prepared for an epidemic of disease than it is for an epidemic of health. So, like much of how great change must come about, it is up to we, the people, to make the biggest change in our health potential and to create a sweeping wave of health across our country. Imagine reading the headline of your local paper that exclaims "Epidemic of health crushes virus," or "America now healthiest country in world."

When it comes to health care, I don't believe in prevention.

I am asked about prevention continuously. When I am talking to groups or doing presentations for companies there will invariably be a question about disease prevention. When

I say, "I don't believe in prevention," the group typically looks at me rather oddly with a what-the-heck-is-he-talking-about expression.

Prevention in health care is a single-bullet idea. Prevention says, "If we do these things, then we can prevent that disease." We can help a woman prevent breast cancer, but still have her die of cardiovascular disease. In the end, has this woman become healthier? No. We prevented the disease that was killing her, without giving her the tools for a healthier lifestyle. Prevention is mechanistic, not holistic; it promotes the idea that if we address one particular issue, then a person is out of the woods. Wouldn't it be better to have that same woman actually become much healthier and adopt a healthier lifestyle than one of disease prevention?

We can treat disease, and we can prevent disease. But we still need to talk about disease of some kind, correct? If we ask how to prevent breast cancer, we stop focusing on being healthy and instead focus on not having cancer.

Although our focus should be the eradication of cancer, we should try to do it by working toward overall health

When people are truly healthy in all aspects—be it physical, nutrient, mental, social, wealth, and spiritual—their longevity greatly increases.

We can either prevent disease or promote health—they are not interchangeable. I choose the latter.

# Chapter 19

# HEALTH IS WHERE THE HEAD IS

Dr. Larry Markson was the founder of a forward-thinking group of chiropractors called the Masters' Circle. Dr. Markson was adamant about the idea of our headspace being the key to success in business.

"It is all in your head." We heard this in nearly every seminar and speech Dr. Markson gave. And he was right. Where our headspace is determines where we will be. If you think you are a business failure, then you will undoubtedly fulfill your prophecy. If you believe we are in slow economic times and nobody can afford your services, then your business will decline. Even if it is untrue, you will act as if it is.

We have had this happen to us in many aspects of our lives. Have you ever gone out on the town one of those nights when you look and feel great? It was a good night wasn't it? Then you wake up another day and say to yourself, *I just know this is going to be a crappy day*. Unless someone knocks at your door with one of those huge Publishers Clearing House checks with your name on it, *I knew it was going to be a bad day*, will keep running through your head.

When it comes to our health, we have some pretty limiting ideas. It seems that we have preconceived ideas about what part of our health  or what particular body part will fail at any given age. I had a twenty-two year old female in my office one day, and I was going through a first day exam with her. I asked her how her health was and she replied, "It's okay."

I said, "But you are twenty-two. What could be wrong with you?"

She looked at me and said, "Well, since I turned twenty my health has just gone downhill!" I almost fell out of my chair. She thought that since she had turned twenty, she was now on the downward slope of life. She had no major life-threatening diseases or failures of organ systems. She was only twenty-two, but she acted like she was 122. I saw seventy year olds that could kick her butt. So what was making her feel that way—her inner monologue. She told herself this was how she was, and that after twenty your health goes downhill.

What would happen if you take a young child and tell him or her on a daily basis that no matter what they do, they will fail in life? We actually see this daily in our office. Some kids succumb to the daily deluge of negativity and end up overwhelmed by the sheer volume of insults. Some kids—I don't know how they do it—take that same crap, turn it around, and become entrepreneurs who make millions and dedicate themselves to making sure no kid has to experience the same thing. Some people let it get fixed in their heads, while others filter it out.

The exact same thing happens with our health. Whoever told us that at some certain age we are bound to be unhealthy? Well, of course if you treat your body poorly for decades, you will end up unhealthy even quicker. You will end up with what Joan Jett titled her fourth album: the Glorious Results of a Misspent Youth.

What if you adopted a belief that you were healthy? What if you adopted a belief that you have an immune system that is like a bullet proof vest? How would you feel? Would you get the flu this year? Chances are that you would most likely not. You believe it you won't get the flu, so you start to act like it is so. You move differently; you think differently, and you are different.

Here is the key: what do you think your healthiest you looks like, acts like, and thinks like is probably much different than you are now. So how can you achieve that better, healthier version of yourself? This is why over half of the people who start a weight loss program say, "this year, I am finally going to lose those pounds and get in shape!" find that after the they drop their New Year's weight loss programs by February first. They have not adopted a healthy head space. They know where the gym is; they know how to use the equipment; and they even know that they will be *so* much better off for exercising. With a laundry list of reasons why they should exercise, they don't. This is all because they have not adopted the "healthiest me" mindset.

"The greatest discovery of any generation is that human beings can alter their lives by altering the attitudes of their minds." —Albert Schweitzer

Dr. Markson would have us write out our "dream practice." This exercise would get us to think about what our ideal practice would look like, feel like, sound like, and even smell like. We would write down in complete detail exactly how our practice would work, down to the very last iota. Most importantly we would state *why* we wanted our practice to be this way. Dr. Markson would advise, "If you have a big enough *why*, the *how* will come."

How could you take this visualization exercise and apply it toward your health? Allow yourself to dream, just for a minute. What does it look like to look, feel, walk, talk, eat, sleep, and think your best? Thinking of the healthiest you for a minute, imagine how you would shop for groceries. How many times would you exercise per week, and what types of exercise would you do? Putting this type of thinking into place sets you apart from where you were only minutes before. This "ideal you" headspace gives you a much different view of yourself and your health potential. Many of the people whom I coach use this exercise to see where they can be health wise.

## Ideal Weight versus Ideal Health

If you really want to make this visualization exercise even more powerful—examine the consequences of not reaching your ideal health. Understanding the fallout will push you to accomplish so much more when you are working toward your ideal health. Realize that it is not reaching your ideal weight, but that it is reaching your ideal *health*. You can easily be an ideal weight and still be unhealthy. Reaching your ideal health includes your ideal weight and so much more.

Dr. Dane Donahue's chiropractic clinic in Newtown, Pennsylvania is the flagship practice for 8 Weeks to Wellness. Dr. Donahue has shown that incredible and life changing steps can be accomplished in only eight weeks. It functions somewhat like the television show, "The Biggest Loser," but in real life. It is amazing. By completing a detailed analysis of his clients' blood work, Dr. Donahue can evaluate patients' health status even if they "feel good." He and his sister and co-owner of 8 Weeks to Wellness, Dr. Denise Chranowski, use the term *skinny fat* to describe people who are at or below their ideal weight, but are nowhere close to being at their ideal health. The blood work of skinny fat people shows that they often have as many elevated markers as obese people would.

Focusing on your ideal weight may not get you to your ideal health; but focusing on your ideal health can get you to your ideal weight. Someone who smokes two packs of cigarettes a day might be at his or her ideal weight, but someone who focuses on reaching his or her ideal health would never smoke those two packs.

It *is* all in your head just as Dr. Markson repeatedly stated. One of the greatest tools you have is the ability to focus your mind on your health. Start today. Ask yourself the following very simple questions and write down the responses you give yourself in detail:

- What does the best me look like, feel, and act like?

- What steps would I take to become the best me?

- What would be the consequences if I do not accomplish this?

- What would be the benefits of accomplishing becoming my best self?

You are much closer to health than you think. It *is* all in your head. So choose a different way of thinking, and you can make it better.

# Chapter 20

# I WOULD TAX SODA.

Cigarettes get taxed more and more each year because we know that down the road, their health care costs will also be massive. Insurance companies have done countless studies comparing the average costs for health care of someone who smokes versus someone who does not. The result: people who smoke will incur much more health care costs than people who don't. With this information in hand, the government takes a pay-to-play approach. If you want to smoke, you have to defray your future health care expenses. It is actually quite simple.

So why doesn't the government tax soda at a similar rate? There are *no* nutritional benefits to soda. It contains artificial taste, artificial coloring, a ton of sugar—usually artificial sugars—and calories galore.

Many schools have strategically gotten rid of soda vending machines. Even when the big two soda companies offer to pay a school district thousands of dollars—maybe even hundreds of thousands of dollars—a year, the school system will say no. They realize that if they take that money, it would be the equivalent of mortgaging students' health for, say, a new football field. And what school district in America couldn't use thousands of extra dollars per year? All they have to do is grant exclusivity to one of the major soda companies. That's it! No competition for the soda company from the other soda company. They know that if they can get to the kids young enough, they will have a customer for life.

New York City Mayor Bloomberg tried to ban large volume soda purchases. I applaud him on the intent, but he had to know that there was no way that would pass. Taxing it would be easier to implement, raise money, and have a bigger impact than banning it. So if we tax all tobacco products because we know the ramifications of smoking, then why wouldn't we do the same for soda? The argument against it is that no research shows that soda is killing thousands of Americans a day. Soda might not be able to kill people by itself, but it sure seems like it is helping. A single can of soda never killed anyone right? Neither does one cigarette. But thirty thousand cigarettes can. This quantity may sound like a lot, but if a person smoked only 8.3 cigarettes per day for ten years, he or she would meet the goal. This is much less than a pack a day.

So how much soda have you drunk in your lifetime?

There are 128 fluid ounces in a gallon. To drink a hundred gallons of soda you would have to drink 12,800 ounces. I know that sounds like an incredible number; but to make that goal, you would have to drink a little over 1,066 twelve-ounce sodas in your lifetime. So if we take the same ten years we did for the smokers, then you would consume just over 106 sodas a year. That would be eight sodas a month or a little over two sodas a week. And that is just over a ten year period. I know people who suck down two, three, or four sodas a day!! It is not uncommon. Now think about doing that for twenty or thirty years. Each American could easily average a couple hundred gallons of soda in his or her lifetime. This is exactly what soda manufacturers want, and I am also sure they do not want you to know just how many sodas—or calories—you drink.

In fact, I think we should tax that entire chip and soda aisle. There is a whole aisle in almost every grocery store in America dedicated to two things: chips and soda. A whole aisle! On the left side is soda and on the right side are the chips. You can go anywhere in America and find this aisle. Not all grocery stores will have many fruit or vegetables, but they will always have a chip and soda aisle.

Tax them. Tax them hard and use that money to lower the prices of fresh fruit and vegetables.

*Chapter 21*

# IS PAIN RELIEF ALL WE REALLY WANT?

Is pain relief what we all really want from our health care system? Several people who come to me for care say that all they want is to be free of pain. Have we been brainwashed into thinking that pain management is the best we can get for so long that it is all we ask for now? We are aiming way too low for our quality of health if we think our whole life is dependent on how much pain we are either in or not in on any given day.

Let's look at it two different ways. First, your body doesn't think pain is as important as you do. Only about 11 percent of the nervous system is dedicated to sensing pain. If I had asked you what percentage of the nervous system was dedicated to pain, you most likely would have said a much higher number. And the neurons that carry pain signals are slower and smaller than the fibers carrying the messages about how you are moving, standing, and sitting. See, your body thinks *that* information is more important. It's not that sensing pain is not an essential part of our nervous system, but only that we should mirror the level of importance our body places on it.

Second, you can be in no pain as well as unhealthy, just like cancer can begin overtaking your body with no pain whatsoever. Chronic diseases often show no pain until the very last stages of the illness, after it has been well entrenched in our bodies. It is typically not until this point that we see pain, and yet the disease may have been around for years.

We can also have pain and be healthy. Have you ever slept funny and woken up in pain or gone for a hike and had sore legs the next day? Sure, we all have; but this does not mean you are unhealthy or have a disease. It actually just means that you are in pain.

What does pain have to do with your health? And the answer is *nothing*.

# Chapter 22

# OUR CHILDREN DESERVE BETTER

Our children deserve better—not more, but better.

- They deserve a planet that will be able to sustain them and not be a source of carcinogens and toxicity that promotes disease and un-health in them.

- The deserve food that is nontoxic, health-promoting, nutritious, affordable, and sustainable.

- They deserve the opportunity for education in numerous subjects and they deserve a level of intellect that won't send them into bankruptcy to acquire.

- They deserve a system that allows them to be healthy and not just un-sick.

- They deserve an opportunity for great health and a map to attaining it.

- They deserve parents who are healthy enough to enjoy their children and their grandchildren; they deserve to have their parents watch them grow, graduate, and step into greatness.

- They deserve parents who by their actions and intentions have mapped out an incredible plan for love, living, and longevity.

- They deserve the chance to have the explosive health that children should have and not be burdened with adult diseases at a young and precious age.

- They deserve the opportunity to communicate one-to-one and face-to-face, and to be able to understand the incredible unspoken words that are said by just looking into the face of someone.

- They deserve more laughter.

- They deserve the opportunity to learn from losing, not from being sheltered; to learn from defeat, not from always winning; to learn from coming in last; and to learn what it is to earn a victory.

- They deserve to be told "I love you" more often.

They deserve not more, but much better.

*Chapter 23*

# WALK, AMERICA!

There doesn't seem to be anyone on the horizon who really wants to tackle the issue of good health. Most elected officials want to dress up the insurance game in different clothes, so it doesn't feel as bad when we pay for our care. But whatever the method of settling up, it is the same game over and over again. It is not *health* care; it is disease treatment and symptom care.

So where do we begin to advocate for our collective health? We start in our elementary schools, of course. We start with mandated physical education classes for every elementary school child, every day of the week. Do you know how many of our states mandate daily physical education classes, not counting recess? Teachers tell me all the time of how some kids will just sit during recess and do not move. Undirected playtime doesn't count. It has to be in a formal gym classroom setting, *every* day.

A few years ago our federal government published exercise guidelines for us. They recommended sixty minutes a day— every day. Americans immediately cried, "We do not have time for sixty minutes every day for exercise!" Soon the papers printed articles that counted mowing the lawn and cleaning the house, among other activities, as exercise, etc. Don't get wrong—yes, they get you moving, yes they are physical, but they are not the same as dedicated exercise time.

It is rather amazing that we read and are told that we need to exercise daily as adults, but we are not told this as kids. We are shown that exercise—PE class—needs to happen only two or three times a week. We can no longer rely on kids to get outside and "play," because they just are not doing that. Time outdoors has been replaced by hours of screen time. So then as adults, it is no wonder that we find it so difficult to shift our mindset to regular exercise, when we have not been programmed to think and act this way.

People often complain that they don't have the energy to exercise. Those of us who exercise regularly know that we actually have more energy when we exercise versus when we do not. It is kind of a mystery that we can work out and get exhausted and yet have more energy.

So why should we start with elementary kids? First of all it is the easiest place to start. The results would be phenomenal and almost immediate. We would see fewer missed days of school and less of a need for medications. Kids would naturally eat better and make better food choices. Test grades would go up. Schools are strapped for time as it is during the day and the school year; regular exercise for students would help them be more attentive and might even help alleviate attention deficit disorder. Children need more stimulation—they need to get moving.

We should then start a national walking club and name it "Walk! America." If Ronald Reagan could make us believe our economy was okay when our auto industry was getting decimated by Japanese car manufacturers in the 1980s, then why can't we have a charismatic leader to get America walking? All that is needed is footwear. We don't need 150-dollar, hi-tech running shoes—just something to get you around the block. And we don't have to walk a marathon—thirty minutes a day will do the trick.

I had one patient in particular who needed to get moving. Her weight was going to be her gateway to numerous diseases. I asked her to start walking thirty minutes a day. She said she couldn't walk that much a day. I said, "Okay, then how about twenty?" She again replied that she was not physically able. We worked our way down to five minutes a day, and she agreed. She really thought that five minutes was all she was physically able to do. And if that *is* all you can do—then do *that*. I told her I wanted her to walk those five minutes every single day. As I had anticipated, she was soon up to over twenty-five minutes a day. She was feeling better, moving better, and her chiropractic adjustments were holding longer, therefore requiring fewer adjustments.

The ad campaign's tagline could be, "Who'd be in yours?" and the commercials would feature regular people on the street being asked, "Who would be in your walking club?" People would have a variety of responses from their moms or the pizza delivery guy to Lou Ferrigno or Michael Jordan. It would be funny and get the message across that we can have fun and get healthier all at the same time.

My walking club would have Oprah, Ben Franklin, my mom, and my wife, Mary, so we could take our greyhounds with us. So who is in yours?

# IT IS NO LONGER JUST ABOUT YOU

Some people have a notion that what they do or how they take care of themselves and their health only affects them. It is true that only you can experience the biggest benefit to your health by being committed to it, but to think that your health does not affect anyone else but you is myopic and selfish.

Have you ever lost a friend or family member? I have lost both my mom and dad. There were people at their funeral masses whom I didn't know. To this day, I will still have people say that they golfed with Dad, played bridge with Mom, or were on committees with one of them and miss them very much. People who worked with them or learned from them will tell me to this day how much they liked my parents.

"We have no idea how far-reaching something we may say, think, or do today will affect the lives of millions tomorrow." —BJ Palmer, DC

We may not fully know the multitudes of lives we have touched; by not being present or by not being at our best, those lives may not be the same. I am not laying on the good Christian guilt for you. It is just true.

Have you ever heard a friend or family member say, "I'm not hurting anyone but me"? They are wrong, aren't they? It hurts you, too, to see them spiral downward. I am not talking just about drug abuse or alcoholism. But what about the people who are morbidly obese, smokers, or people with low self-esteem? The list could go on, but all of these people behave in ways that negatively impact others as well as themselves.

Maybe we are scared to tell those people how much we care, and that there will also be a little bit of us missing when they are no longer here. Maybe we should tell them that it does hurt to see them slowly fade. So although it may be selfish on our parts to think of our own feelings after they are gone, maybe it is also okay for love to be selfish.

Wouldn't you want to play more golf with them? Wouldn't you want to play with your kids or grandkids a bit more? Maybe you wanted to go scuba-diving or take your special person dancing one more time without caring one ounce if anyone was watching at all. Or maybe you wanted to sit with your best friend and catch the Yankees a couple of more times.

How special would it be to spend just that much more time with the people you know and love? How wonderful to spend just a little bit longer with them and to bask in the warmth of the sunshine that is your time together? So it is not about just you. It is about us.

It is about how we are affected by you being here. It is about how we plan time to be with you. It is about how the words you have spoken to us could have never been spoken so directly to our hearts by anyone else.

We are affected by you. We are affected by just knowing that you are an e-mail or phone call away, and that makes all the difference in the world.

And we want more.

# REFERENCES

1.  Marmot MG, Syme SL., *Acculturation and coronary heart disease in Japanese-Americans,* Am J Epidemiol. 1976 Sep;104(3):225-47.

2.  John EM, Phipps AI, Davis A, Koo J., *Migration history, acculturation, and breast cancer risk in Hispanic women,* Cancer Epidemiol Biomarkers Prev. 2005 Dec;14(12):2905-13.

3.  HELEN P. HAZUDA1, STEVEN M. HAFFNER1, MICHAEL P. STERN1 and CLAYTON W. EIFLER2 + Author Affiliations, *EFFECTS OF ACCULTURATION AND SOCIOECONOMIC STATUS ON OBESITY AND DIABETES IN MEXICAN AMERICANS*

THE SAN ANTONIO HEART STUDY, Oxford Journals Medicine American Journal of Epidemiology Volume 128, Issue 6Pp. 1289-1301.

4.  http://www.who.int/universal_health_coverage/en/

5.  http://www.cdc.gov/dhdsp/data_statistics/fact_sheets/fs_men_heart.htm

6.  http://www.cdc.gov/dhdsp/data_statistics/fact_sheets/fs_women_heart.htm

7.  http://www.health.gov/paguidelines/factsheetprof.aspx

8.  Kado DM, Huang MH, Karlamangla AS, Barrett-Connor E, Greendale GA,
    *Hyperkyphotic posture predicts mortality in older community-dwelling men and women: a prospective study*, J Am Geriatr Soc. 2004 Oct;52(10):1662-7.

9.  Griegel-Morris P, Larson K, Mueller-Klaus K, Oatis CA, *Incidence of common postural abnormalities in the cervical, shoulder, and thoracic regions and their association with pain in two age groups of healthy subjects.* Phys Ther. 1992 Jun;72(6):425-31.

10. Gerloff P,Ed.D., "*The Possibility Paradigm*", Psychology Today, June 21, 2011.

11. Berk RA, Ph.D., *'Does Humor in course tests reduce anxiety and improve test performance?',* College Teaching, 48, 151-158, 2000.

Made in United States
North Haven, CT
18 May 2023

36729027R10069